What People Are Saying About Demystified . . .

"Here is the short and sweet summary - this works!

When I first started out, I had a business website but even if you typed in my company name, my website didn't come up on Google until about page 10. After applying Markus' principles, a Google search for the keywords related to my industry brought up my website on the first page, just below the paid listings.

The ideas here seemed a little daunting when I read them. Let's face it, a small business owner doesn't have time or money to spare. These activities didn't cost my company anything, and I was able to cover what needed to be done for a month in a couple of hours.

The book is an easy read, and it is effective and useful information."

Sherri Gallagher

President, Technacon Company Inc

"I've worked with Markus for close to 4 years and just like his work, his book is easy to understand, gets results & over delivers. Yia Sou"

Jim Lappas

Owner of Fodrak's Restaurant

"I have read Markus' book and found it to be incredibly informative and beneficial. Once establishing our keywords, we implemented search engine optimization techniques learned from his book and obtained immediate results. In one amazing example, we went from a ranking of 72 on Google to a ranking of 3. In supplementary keywords, we continue to "climb the proverbially Google ladder" as well. We desire to continue to dominate our market share in our industry and with what we have learned in Demystified, we can continue to increase our business in this arena."

Jay Cash

Principle, Sign-A-Rama, Libertyville, Illinois

"If you are like I was: confused and uncertain about online marketing; wary of throwing money into a project with dubious results; and trying to apply good business sense and practices to your online marketing initiatives – then this book is for you. Markus provides you with an understandable, step-by-step business approach to online marketing."

Dan Kreutzer
Author, *Put the WIN back in Your Sales*

DEMYSTIFIED

The Business Owner's Roadmap to More
Customers, Clients and Patients Online.

The offer on page 87 is open to all purchasers of Demystified - The Business Owner's Roadmap to More Customers, Clients and Patients Online by Markus K. Loving. Original proof of purchase is required. The offer is limited to DemystifiedBookOnline.com membership training site only, and your registration for the membership training site is subject to availability of space and changes to the program. Corporate or organizational purchaser may not use one book to invite more than two people. While participants will be responsible for registering with accurate information and any other costs, the initial three months of membership is complimentary. Participants in the membership site are under no additional financial obligation whatsoever to DemystifiedBookOnline.com or Markus K. Loving for the first three months of membership. Registration on the membership site must be completed by August 31, 2016.

Any mention of earnings or income should not be construed as representative of fixed or standard earnings. This book nor the membership training site is not intended to provide personalized legal, accounting, financial, or investment advice. Readers are encouraged to seek the counsel of competent professionals regarding such matters. The Author and Publisher specifically disclaim any liability, loss, or risk that is incurred as a consequence, directly or indirectly, of the use and application of any of the contents of this work.

Demystified

*The Business Owner's Roadmap to More Customers,
Clients and Patients Online.*

ISBN: 978-0692577608

1. Business & Economics / Marketing / General
First Paperback Edition

For more information on using the Internet to get more customers, clients and patients, call Online Market Domination at (847) 238-2768
or visit OnlineMarketDomination.com

This book is dedicated to
my beautiful & loving wife,
my brilliant & amazing daughter,
all the entrepreneurs and business owners
who keep this country great and prosperous,
and to this amazing universe we live in.

You All Rock My World!

TABLE OF CONTENTS

PART ONE

YOUR CUSTOMERS, CLIENTS AND PATIENTS ARE LOOKING FOR YOU ONLINE...WILL THEY FIND YOU?

PART TWO
GET RANKED...GET FOUND...GET BUSINESS

PART THREE
ONLINE MARKET DOMINATION MADE EASY

Acknowledgments...

I have a lot of people to thank for getting me to this point in my career, encouraging me as well as holding me accountable for completing this work.

To those who believed in me in the early days and gave me guidance and business sense when I really didn't have much, Jeff Capitel, Alan Poms, Bob Middleton, David & Debbie Reeder, Ken & Sandi Burgess and Steven Goldberg.

To my best friends since grade school, Pete Dykas and Eric Mueller.

My Fraternity brothers, Tom Caruso, Chris McMillan, Mike Neary, Thor Peplow, Kevin McArdle, Mike Ellis and Vic Mattison.

My most loyal clients and colleagues: BEG Advisors, Navratan Gems, SENG Peers, Jim Lappas, Sherri Gallagher, John Zack, Kevin Purcell, Master Brian Van Patten, April & Chad Toney, Dan Kreutzer, Bob Lambert, Anup Manchanda, Mario Feijoo, Steve Feltner, Nick Bello, Dr. Dan Vander Weit and Dr. Dave Williams.

To the many fellow comrades in my industry who don't even realize how much they impact my business as they motivate me, share their knowledge & tools with me and make me a better online marketer and strategist: Martin Maybruck, Sam Clarke, Brian Anderson, David Sprague, Syd Michaels, Jeff Hopp, Jack Mize, Brian Horn, Sue White & Jeanne Kolenda, Derral Eves, Dr Dan & Ben Littlefield, Brian Parnell and Paul James. And I can't leave out the many inspirational writers who have shared their wisdom to guide me to reach for the best version of myself: Jim Rohn, Tony Robbins, Wayne Dyer, James Redfield, Neale Donald Walsch and Rhonda Byrne.

My mom, who left me too early yet instilled in me a passion for life, a strong work ethic, and self-reliance that only a single mother can do.

To my dad & step-mom for always being there for me, cheering me on during the good times and encouraging me through the tough times

To Marianne, the best mother-in-law a guy could ask for.

My cousin Kristi who I probably wouldn't have made it through my teenage years without.

To my grandma Irene, who always saw the greatness in me and taught me so much about life and the world around me. My grandpa Walter, who was tough on me, yet gave me gifts and life lessons that still shape my life's philosophy. And my Vanaema & Vanaisa (that's grandma and grandpa in Estonian) who were always there for me and looked out for me when I needed it most.

And most of all, to the two most important women in my life, my loving wife & life partner and my amazing daughter, who are always there for me and support me unconditionally. KK you always give me the creative space I need and put up with all my wild and crazy ideas, passions, dreams and hearts desires. Most of all, you've always got my back. Thank you! And to my brilliant daughter who rocks my world and inspires me to be a better person! You see the love in this world and all its wonder and possibilities! I love you both so very very much! You are my life and inspire me more than you'll ever know!!!

Foreword

Dear Business Reader,

No one disputes that the proliferation of the Internet throughout society has altered our behavior in almost every aspect of our lives. For the business community, this has resulted in dramatic changes in how customers approach the marketplace and make buying decisions. The combination of these two factors has thrown businesses a real curve ball. How do you adapt and cope with the new market realities? Failure to do so successfully will most likely have catastrophic consequences for the business.

When the Internet first rose to prominence, virtually every business jumped on board and built a website because it was the thing to do. Conventional wisdom told us that it would do great things for our businesses – but we didn't know. Unfortunately in most cases, as is the case with new technology, the results achieved fell far short of expectations.

Most websites were little more than the company's marketing brochure converted from print to digital format. They were passive because they were built from a base that was designed for a passive medium. The result was that most websites were not designed to interact with the customer – the key component of the Internet. Sadly, most websites still fall into this category – they occupy cyberspace but do little for the companies they represent.

As search engines evolved, they became the most critical factor in how customers found and purchased products and services. Unless the customer was specifically looking for your business by name (highly unlikely), the probability that a passive website would show up in the customer's search results was virtually nil. They can't buy from you if they don't know you exist!

If the Internet didn't already confound you with e-commerce and online marketing, you almost certainly were when social media jumped into the mix! Once again, the siren's call of explosive business potential filled the air.

We are constantly regaled with the expectation of unlimited potential for our businesses. But for most business owners, this sounds all too familiar – especially if you're still waiting to reap the benefits promised by the initial website initiatives. No doubt you're more than a little reluctant to plunge into this brave new world.

As a business owner, one of my greatest frustrations was engaging with Internet "experts" that were technologists, not business people. Every one offered me a different opinion, most of which conflicted with one another. Business results, if considered at all, were framed in nebulous and generic terms. The focus seemed to be on various esoteric approaches and technical features that, quite frankly, I didn't understand, and even if I did, I had no discernible connection that I was able to make to my business objectives.

Then I met Markus.

He approached the situation from a business perspective. Technology was a tool to be utilized to achieve business goals. He spoke in business-oriented English, not the usual technobabble I had come to expect. For the first time, I was able to connect the dots between this technology and tangible business results.

If you are like I was: confused, uncertain, and wary of throwing money into a project with dubious results; and trying to apply good business sense and practices to online marketing initiatives – then this book is for you. It will provide you with an understandable, step-by-step business approach to online marketing.

As you embark on your journey into the dark and foreboding region of cyberspace called online marketing, I can think of no better guide than Markus.

Sincerely,
Daniel W. Kreutzer

Managing Partner
Samurai Business Group, LLC

Author of *Put the WIN back in Your Sales, Buyer Process Management* and *Essential Sales Management*

(312) 863-8580

d.kreutzer@samuraibizgrp.com

www.SamuraiBizGrp.com

Creating Competitive Advantage through Sales Team Effectiveness™

Introduction

Webster says Demystified means "to make (something) clear and easy to understand: to explain (something) so that it no longer confuses or mystifies someone."

I like Google's definition Demystified: make (a difficult or esoteric subject) clearer and easier to understand. "This book attempts to demystify technology" (Google)

I wrote this book to remove the mystery that seems to be looming when it comes to marketing your business online. I can't tell you how many times I hear; "It seems so complicated", "Where do I start", "Should I be on Facebook, Google+, LinkedIn? How about video and mobile?", "What about reviews?", I could go on and on.

The truth is, like many industries out there, the insiders and "professionals" want you to feel that way because they feel it gives them more control or "job security". Some might even say it gives them a sense of power. My whole goal with Demystified – The Business Owner's Roadmap to More Customers, Clients and Patients Online., is to shatter that myth and give you the roadmap and some tools you need to do this for your business. To get more customers, clients, patients, readers, whoever your target audience is, from the Internet.

That is if you choose to.

See, the question shouldn't be can you do this. Of course, you can. You're smart enough. You've obviously got the drive to start and run your own business. There's no question; You CAN do it.

No. The real question is… Should you? Should you spend the most precious resource, any of us has, our time on learning to market yourself online or is it more prudent for you to spend your time on your core competency – your business?

Or could there be some balance in between?

Jim Rohn, one of my early mentors, said it best, "If it's easy to do, it's easy not to do." My intention is that by the time you finish reading Demystified – The Business Owner's Roadmap to More Customers, Clients and Patients Online., you'll understand this "mystery" of successful Internet marketing and have a firm grasp on what needs to be done to increase your ROI. If this book had eyes where I could see you finish it, I'd love to see you breathing a sigh of relief realizing that this is easy to do.

Now please don't misunderstand what I'm saying here. Even though marketing yourself online is easy, this won't be quick to do or happen overnight. Nothing worth doing ever is. It takes work and time to implement your online business plan. It will take patience to dominate your market online. And it takes your willingness to learn and implement. So, if you're up to the task and willing to do a little bit every day (easy to do), you'll be well on your way to getting more business online.

In the pages ahead, I'm giving you the road map of what needs to be done. Think of this book as your playbook, your Online Business Plan if you will. And with my special gift to you at the end of this book, I'm giving you the tools to implement that plan.

Now it's up to you!

Wishing you all the very best-

Part One

Your Customers, Clients, and Patients
Are Looking For You Online...
Will They Find You?

CHAPTER 1

Online Marketing for Local Business

If you are the owner of a local business, you are probably suffering from a drop in demand for your products or services as a result of the economic recession. Most areas have been suffering from the recession for the past few years. In fact, even with the "recovery", statistics show that small local businesses are making 30% to 50% less than they were just a few years ago. Some of the businesses that comprise this statistic include:

- Dentists

- Plumbers

- Attorneys

- Locksmiths

- Restaurants

- Plastic Surgeons

- Accountants

- Carpet Cleaners

- Contractors

- Landscapers

- (Insert Your Industry Here)

Traditional Marketing Doesn't Work Anymore

The fact of the matter is that most of the marketing techniques that were solid and reliable to local businesses to use to reach their market in the past are no longer working. Old marketing techniques, such as *Yellow Pages* ads, newspapers and other types of hard copy advertising are simply not bringing in business like they once did. That's because people simply don't use them anymore.

Businesses that are still using such outdated forms of advertising are throwing away thousands and thousands of dollars on ineffective marketing every month. If you are one of those people still investing in such ads, ask ten people where their copy of the *Yellow Pages* is. Most can't tell you or will tell you they put it in the recycling bin shortly after it arrived. What does that tell you about the money you're spending?

Consumers are looking more and more to the Internet to find information about the services and products they are seeking, even locally. For this reason, if businesses want to reach new customers they simply must have a quality Internet presence. And that does not mean just a lame website that a kid could have put together!

Today's most effective websites are well thought out, interesting, personable and informative. They utilize a variety of savvy online marketing techniques in order to stand out from their competitors. If you have a site with no keywords in it and almost no quality backlinks and, more importantly, no citations, especially from authority sites, you are missing the boat. You will never get to the top of the search engine results without them.

Specific Marketing Strategies

There are specific marketing strategies that apply uniquely to dominating your market online. If you're not staying on top of these Internet marketing strategies and implementing them, your website will not get traffic, and you'll miss out on one of the most efficient and lucrative sources of new customers for your business.

One of the stumbling blocks keeping most local business owners from using online marketing strategies to grow their customer base is that they simply have no idea what to do. Online marketing is so new, always changing and evolving and such unfamiliar territory for most business owners that they don't know where to start. They spend so much time running their business, taking care of their customers and managing their staff that they don't have the time to learn something new – especially something that's constantly evolving.

Ask yourself a few questions:

- What are long-tail keywords?

- What is keyword density?

- What is Web 2.0?

- What's a citation?

- What's a Google Hangout?

- How do you create quality backlinks?

- How do you set up an autoresponder?

- How do you change the tags on your website?

- How do you get quality reviews and more importantly where should they go?

- How do you create videos and audios for your website and social media pages?

If you're like most business owners, you can't answer these questions with much certainty. That is normal. You've wisely spent your time focusing on other aspects of your business – the ones that were crucial for you to master. But now you need to learn more! Finally, the time has come for average local business owners to discover what they need to do to put an online marketing plan effectively in place for their businesses.

Changes in Business

Today, most local business owners are running lean and hungry. They need more work and more customers coming through their door. They need to adapt to the changing economy. Today's business environment is in constant flux – specifically, the whole process of reaching your target market cost-effectively is nothing like it was even a decade ago. Understanding these changes and meeting the challenges they present is essential to the survival of your business.

Case in point: One local business was spending $8,000 per month on *Yellow Pages* advertising that cost more than it was bringing in. It doesn't take long before smart business people recognize this as fighting a losing battle, a big problem that needs to be fixed. So they stopped the ad. However, now they have an $8,000 budget for marketing but don't know what to do to get the best possible return on their marketing investment. Because they don't know Internet marketing, they could easily pour those funds into online strategies that either falls flat or backfire. The learning curve is sharp and unforgiving.

But these entrepreneurs realize the Internet is the future. More than 30 billion local searches are performed online every month. This number grows by more than 50% each year. In fact, 83% of people search online before they make a purchase. Even more important, the vast majority of searchers look online for local services and products before they make a buying decision. They now prefer this type of search over *Yellow Pages* or the newspaper. For this reason, business owners need to be online in an effective way.

The Potential for Exponential Profit Growth

Effective Internet marketing can easily result in an increase in sales of tens of thousands of dollars. This is amazing considering the sheer number of layoffs, crises, and more that people are facing. The old ways of getting business in the door don't work ,and they have to learn something new. Many people who thought they retired find themselves just a couple of years later back in their business working hard. They are the people who can use Internet marketing and an online business plan to save their business and their livelihood.

By putting effective online marketing strategies to work, you are not only positively impacting your own business, you are improving your local economy. More money is being spent locally, especially with the advent of the Shop & Support Local movement over the last few years. With a steady stream of new customers flowing into your sales funnel, downsizing and layoffs become a thing of the past. In fact, your business will grow, despite the economy because you are reaching those who are looking to buy from businesses like yours. And that is what effective marketing is all about!

Online marketing has the potential for exponential profit growth. If you are not ready for your business to double or grow even more, stop reading now!

Statistics You Need to Know

The following statistics give you a glimpse of how people are using the Internet to find the products and services they need:

- 64% of U.S. Gross Domestic Product comes from local businesses.

- 4.2 million local small businesses have sales in the $500,000 to $20,000,000 range.

- Over 30 billion local searches are performed monthly – a number that grows more than 50% each year.

- 98% of searchers choose a business that is on page 1 of the results they get.

- More searches are being done on mobile devices than desktop/laptop computers.

- In mobile, between 40% and 50% of search queries carry a local intent

- 72% of buyers trust reviews as much as personal recommendations.

- Consumers will choose a business with seven 5-star reviews over a higher ranked business with fewer reviews

- 56% of clicks go to the #1 ranked site in a search.

- 13.5% of clicks go to the #2 ranked site in a search.

- 10% of clicks go to the #3 ranked site in a search.

These statistics show how important it is for your business to develop and implement an online marketing strategy. A solid online marketing strategy can catapult your business to the top of the search engine results so when a prospective customer searches for you (without knowing your name or business name) they find you. And then from that point, to build a 5-star reputation so that when they find you, they will trust you to buy.

Making Changes to Your Online Methods

Like most businesses, you probably need to make some pretty drastic changes to your marketing plans to maximize the results you get from online marketing. Here are some insider facts you need to know about marketing your business online:

- The potential to grow your business using online marketing is phenomenal, no matter what industry. You just need to cultivate the opportunity.

- There are seven extremely useful Internet marketing techniques that no one is doing. Learn them and put them into practice, and you will outperform all your competitors quickly.

- You need to achieve local online market domination, a goal you can reach by learning and mastering a five-step process. Following these steps correctly virtually guarantees you'll get the results you want.

- Creating and following a proven online business plan is essential to managing all the crucial tasks needed to get to the top of the search results and get more new customers into your business.

- Establishing a baseline is critical before you implement a new marketing plan. Take the time to analyze thoroughly what you are already doing and what you need to change so you can measure your progress.

- Make your tasks more reasonable by breaking them down. Start with the tasks that are one-time jobs, as they provide the foundation for your marketing plan, and you will have the pleasure of checking things off your list.

- Only when you finish the one-time tasks should you begin the tasks that repeat. These are long-term commitments that will require monthly, weekly or even daily attention.

- You should consider seeking out Internet marketing partner(s) for a portion of or the entire online business plan, for the sake of expediency and skill. There are many who can take on select tasks to facilitate the process for you.

- Create a system for tracking the results from implementing your marketing plan. Measure the increase in your business income.

CHAPTER 2

Seven Strategies No One's Doing

While some people are using select Internet marketing techniques to drive traffic to their site, others are doing nothing at all, except hoping for the best. Using a wide variety of tried and true online marketing methods is the best way to see real results in your sales. A great place to start is by opting to implement the seven strategies practically no one is doing. These strategies produce serious results and should be used by every business with an Internet presence. They include:

- Blogging

- Autoresponders - building an email list and following up

- Complimentary or Free Reports

- Online Video

- Reputation Marketing

- Mobile Optimized Marketing

- Basic SEO (Search engine optimization)

Blogging

Blogging creates a steady online presence that increases your chances of being at the top of search engine results for your keywords. Using a blog you can generate the content containing all your long-tail keywords on the web. In addition, it allows you to build a following of customers and potential customers who are interested in what you share and who provide valuable feedback to you. This audience is ripe for being marketed to when your business is in a slump.

Autoresponders

These are tools that allow you to build an email list and easily follow up with those on it. They are a set of standardized letters that you set up once, and the necessary contact with each new individual who opts into your email list is taken care of automatically. An autoresponder is an indispensable tool that saves time for you and actually does some of the lead nurturing that is essential in demand marketing.

Offering Complimentary or Free Reports

Providing these reports to those who are interested is another of the underused tools in the online marketer's toolbox. Everyone loves getting something for nothing. If you offer free reports on an area of interest to your potential customers, you will establish yourself as an expert in that field, and you will easily be able to get them to give their email or other contact information in exchange for a report that actually provides useful information.

Online Video

Online video is the video version of blogs, articles, and reviews. You can reach numerous customers and potential customers with this new hot online marketing tool. You can create a simple video from text slides and voiceover or music, or you can record a video of actual products and services in use. Be sure to place video both on your site and offsite for maximum effectiveness.

Reputation Marketing

This is where you proactively build and market a 5-Star reputation within online directories such as Yelp, Merchant Circle, City Search; social sites like Facebook, Google+ and LinkedIn and your website(s) and blogs. With 80 million Google+ pages merging with each company's website that reveals the company's reputation to their searchers, customer reviews are now a major factor in dominating your market because your online reputation now shows up virtually everywhere.

Mobile Optimized Marketing

This relatively new platform goes unused by those looking to promote their business online because they don't realize how important having a dedicated mobile website is. These sites are built on a mobile platform and link to your main website (ex. m.yourdomain.com). They automatically detect what kind of device your customer is searching on and then dish out the correct version of your website. These mobile optimized sites are what Google and the other search engines are not only looking for but are demanding because so many searches are now done on mobile devices. It's making sure that your mobile website loads fast and is easy to navigate on a mobile device as well as has the desired features your mobile customers are looking for, such as touch to call and one-click directions.

Basic SEO or Search Engine Optimization

SEO is another tool that goes unused by those looking to promote their business online. It is simply making sure that your website is as appealing as possible to the spiders that crawl the Internet collecting information for search engines. This information includes strategic use of keywords, quality backlinks and more.

Many businesses pay a lot of money to have someone create a fancy looking website for them, but it simply is not search engine optimized, so it will never get ranked in the search engine results. Without the strategic use of keywords and phrases, a significant number of quality links to their site and the removal of sluggish and outdated elements like Flash, a website will never achieve a top ranking. This also includes SEO for your mobile site.

By putting in place these seven strategies that not many businesses are doing, you will be able to set your website easily apart from that of most of your competitors. Your search engine rankings will begin to climb quickly, and you will find that more and more customers are "stumbling across" your website.

CHAPTER 3

Online Local Market Domination

While it sounds rather ominous, online local market domination is what you want for your business in order to be a huge success. Online local domination means that you are the number one authority online for your local market. You get that distinction by taking your business from hard-to-find online to being everywhere online. You will be in the top 10 of the local search, natural search and pay-per-click (PPC) campaigns. Your content will show up in top results, and you will have more consumer reviews than any other local business in your market.

When your business is consistently the most popular one found in any online search, and you are absolutely everywhere your local customers look, potential new customers quickly come to recognize that you are the authority in your field. They will want to do business with you because they will recognize you as the best. And who doesn't want to do business with the best?

Online local market domination is simply being the most readily found business of its type in a given local area. If your business is consistently at the top of local search results, normal search results and geo-targeted generic results, you have achieved online local domination. If your business is at the top of normal search results not including an indicator of the area, it is even better.

You can make yourself the master of local results by understanding how searches work. You need to understand the different keywords that individuals use to search for businesses like yours. Understanding how search works will help you employ different online marketing techniques to help you effectively get to the top of the search engine results, exactly where you want to be.

Page 1 results are what you need and ultimately what matter most because 98% of people search and choose from the page 1 results, no matter what search engine they use. In fact, you want to be in the top three results for your keywords in order to get potential customers to your site. If you are not in those results, you are losing out on a lot of business.

Professional online marketers can get most businesses to number one in the search results for local keywords on Google within a month or two. Obtaining a number one position for local keywords is possible because most of them have very little competition and are, for this reason, ripe for someone with knowledge to come around.

The 5 Foundational Keys to Online Market Domination

Start the 5 point online market domination process today in order to achieve online local domination. You can be everywhere you want to be online by using:

- Local business results (Google My Business Pages)
- Natural search results
- PPC results
- Content results
- Mobile Results

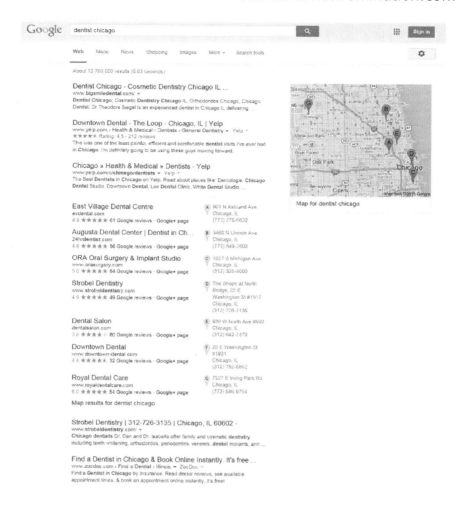

Local Search Results — Google My Business Local Pages

One of the components of online market domination is being prominent among the local business results in Google My Business (formally Google+ Local and Google Places) Pages. Google My Business Pages is an interactive way for people to find local businesses and, best of all, it is an opportunity for a local business to be featured on page one of Google.

Google My Business Pages, which replaced Google + Local, is an important tool for businesses to know and understand so they can use it successfully to market and grow their business online. Google My Business Pages can help businesses rank higher in organic search results, but maybe more importantly, Google My Business Pages can help a business rank higher in local search results.

Google My Business Pages works in connection with Google's social media platform Google+. In fact, every Google+ profile has a toolbar to the left of the home page that has a button labeled "local." This button is simply another way for others to find a local business. So, any business that has taken the initiative to register with Google My Business can see their business prominently displayed when using the "local" button . Having a local business found in this manner is in addition to being able to be found via mobile apps or through an online search at Google.com or Google Maps.

Google ranks Google My Business Pages results on three factors:

- Relevance: If someone searches for a dry cleaner in Chicago, then only dry cleaners will show up vs. other types of businesses in the area.

- Distance: Google will provide search results based on the general location entered by a searcher or based on the distance between the location of a searcher and a local business.

- Prominence: How well-known is the business? Google uses resources throughout the web and provides search results based on how well-known that business is, including reviews.

Google My Business Page's prominence is enhanced when those using a local business' services leave plenty of positive reviews. The star rating system Google uses changed after they acquired Zagat, and now anyone with a Google+ account can write a review based on a 30-point Zagat scoring system. The scoring system helps Google rate a local business. For this reason, the better the business' Zagat ratings, the better the business' rank on Google.

The key to making the most of a Google My Business Page listing is to complete the business profile entirely, accurately, and consistently. Customer reviews are a vital part of creating a complete profile on Google My Business Pages, and the more interactive you are with

Google+ the more you can expect positive reviews, at least by those in your circles.

More Local Search Results

Even though Google has an 80% share of the search market, you don't want to forget about Yahoo & Bing, because let's face it, 20% of 1.5+ Billion searches is still a lot of searches. These are the local business map listings that are at the top above natural search results when you search a keyword in Yahoo! and Bing. You must take the initiative to get listed there. Make sure your business comes up for a variety of keyword phrases, as well as for variations on your business name. And make sure your business name, address and phone number appear **exactly** as you have it on your Google My Business page.

Natural Search Results

The natural search results are those organic results that are generated by search engine searches and are listed directly below the sponsored ads and the local search results. In addition to your actual website, other things can appear in the natural search results. For this reason you need to pay attention to the use of keywords in the following, because they are all commonly found ranked in natural search results:

- Articles
- Videos
- Off-site blogs
- Press releases
- Social networking profiles
- Social bookmarking profiles

Pay-Per-Click Results

Sponsored results or pay-per-click results, are instant exposure for your business. They appear at the very top of search results, as well as to the right of results. A carefully written ad can give great results in converting site visitors into customers. Be sure to make a budget for

PPC ads and stick to it because it can get out of hand. And now with being able to place PPC ads in Facebook, Gmail & even LinkedIn, it's the fastest way to get traffic to your site, PPC is an important online marketing strategy and a valuable part of your online business plan.

Content Results

Online market domination comes when your content is in the top results of a search for your keywords. For example, if someone searches for a given keyword that you use in your online marketing strategy, and the top five results returned are your business website ranked number one, one of your videos ranked number four and one of your press releases ranked number five, chances are you will be recognized as the online authority by searchers. This means the potential client is very likely to choose your business over another to meet its needs.

Getting this type of result is easy to do because Google loves content from Web 2.0 applications, like online articles, press releases and videos. If your content is out there on authority sites and presented in an SEO format, you will find that getting multiple places at the top of a search is the norm.

Mobile Results

Mobile results are the content that Google or the other search engines dish up when customers are searching for a business on their smartphone. In fact, 1 out of every three customers find the business on their mobile phone. In 2014, more than 50% of searches were conducted on a mobile device, according to Google. That content needs to be mobile friendly. Meaning that your website is easy to use and navigate with the customer in mind.

Here's what Google has to say in their Mobile Playbook…

"At Google, we believe that now is the time to close that knowing versus doing gap. It is time to take action and not just do mobile, but do mobile right."

You can learn more about Google's guidelines, suggestions and things to consider regarding mobile at www.themobileplaybook.com.

As you can see, with the use of the foundational 5 key point online market domination model, you will be able to get the outstanding results for which you are looking.

CHAPTER 4

Your Simple Online Business Plan

An online business plan is a must! In order to succeed you need to have a structured plan and work through it, knowing what exactly needs to be done. Below is a simple roadmap for you to follow which you can put in place for your business:

- Identify your ideal customers and what keywords they use to search.

- Use personal branding to gain trust in the online marketplace.

- Optimize your website layout and use search engine optimization.

- Start the 5-point online market domination (use local business results, natural search results, PPC results and content results).

- Get ranked in the local business results.

- Get in all the online business directories.

- Use all of the "local sites" to get tons of quality links that equals high natural search results.

- Utilize simple article marketing.

- Have a blog and consistently make posts using "long tail" keywords to improve your ranking on the search engines.

- Have a dedicated Mobile optimized website

- Create Internet videos and put them on your site and distribute to video sites.

- Create Internet audios and put them on your site and distribute on audio/podcast sites.

- Build a 5-star reputation on all the major online review and social media sites.

- Compose online press releases.

- Make use of PPC by using targeted "local" keywords and geo-targeting "generic" keywords.

- Monitor and optimize how much traffic is getting to your site, how many new customers are being converted from that traffic, how keywords ranked and what has been done to cause these changes.

- Apply social media and social networking techniques.

- Use local discussion forums.

- Use classified ad sites like Craigslist.

- Set up an autoresponder and build an email list for your business (get the power of "Customers and Cash on Demand!")

- Make sure your website and other online assets are mobile optimized and mobile searcher centric.

Prior to Putting Your Online Business Plan in Place

Before you begin putting your new online business plan in place, you should analyze what exactly you have done to date in terms of your website and online marketing and, therefore, what is most pressing. You cannot achieve everything at once, so by being thorough about it, you can effectively spot where best to begin. Evaluate your current status so you get a clear, up-to-date picture of where you are starting from, where you want to go and what must be done to get there.

Analyze Your Overall Online Marketing Strategy

Ask yourself the following questions about your current online marketing:

- How do you market your company?

- How do you promote your web presence already?

- Do you use pay-per-click ads?

- How much do you spend on those ads? Are they working?

- How many unique visitors does your site get per month?

- What type of training does your sales team undergo?

- Why do you want to put an online marketing plan in place?

- What is the value of your average sale?

- Are you capable of exponential growth?

- What percentage of your revenues comes from leads generated by the Internet?

- How many sales/leads do you get per month from your website?

- What traffic techniques do you currently use to drive traffic to your website?

- How much are you currently spending each month to get that traffic?

- What is the average revenue per sale?

- What is the average profit per sale?

- On average, how often does a customer buy from you?

- Approximately how many current customers do you have?

- Approximately how many customers have ever bought from you?

- Do you periodically touch base with them? If so, how often and how?

- How many reviews do I have?

- Are these reviews online? If so, on what sites?

- Do I have offline written testimonies?

- Does my team know how to proactively ask for reviews?

At the end of these questions, you should have a good report card on the overall health of your Internet business plan as it now is for your business. The answers to the above questions will let you know if it is working or not. It also starts to uncover some of the potential for growth that your business has!

Analyze Your Online Business Plan for Each Line

For each specific service or product, you offer, ask the question:

- Do you target local business results on Google?
- Are you registered with the online local business directories?
- Do you use search engine optimization to show up for the natural search results?
- Do you use article marketing?
- Do you have a blog? If so, how often do you post?
- Do you have videos on your site?
- Do you use videos on YouTube and other locations to promote your site?
- Do you use online press releases?
- Do you use pay-per-click?
- Is my website mobile friendly and optimized?
- Do you test and track your main web pages?
- Do you use online classified ad sites?
- Do you use online local forums?
- Do you use audio marketing on your site and also syndicate the audio on other popular sites?
- Do you use email list building on your website?
- Do you have reviews online?
- Do I have a consistent system to collect online reviews?

All of the above methods should be in place in order to effectively market your business through your website. In fact, most of these things should be done for each of the different product lines or services you carry. This is especially true if you target different markets, like residential and commercial. You need different approaches to reach each one, and while you may send them back to the same site, your pay-per-click campaign, landing pages, online classified ads, local forums, email lists, videos, audios, articles, reviews, and blogs should be tailored to each market.

Part Two

Get Ranked… Get Found… Get Business!

CHAPTER 5

Where to Begin

If you're looking for the overall job of setting an effective online marketing plan in place for your business, it seems rather daunting. However, if you look more closely at the list of online marketing tasks there are many things that will make a difference to your strategy and they are just one-time tasks. Start with them. Make sure you keep track of when they are completed to ensure you haven't missed something very important.

The one-time tasks that you must begin include:

- Find your ideal customers.
- Do detailed keyword research.
- Do onsite search engine optimization updates.
- Add a lead capture system to your website.
- Do personal branding changes.

Set yourself a deadline for the completion of these tasks. While these things are essential to increasing your online presence, if you just do them alone it will take a long time to rise through the search results, if at all. These tasks are the foundation of your marketing plan. Without them, many of your other strategies will fail, so they are very important to do and to do well. However, don't simply do these and then stop.

Finding the Ideal Customer

Finding the ideal customer for your business is a one-time job. You probably think that any customer at all is ideal. However, there are some that are much better than others. Knowing how to identify them and who to stay away from will make your business run more smoothly. In addition, your marketing campaign will be much more effective because you will be able to target that customer precisely with the very keywords they use when they search for goods and services.

In order to uncover your ideal customer, you will need to conduct keyword research by analyzing the different markets that you serve. This will also help you to determine which niches you should target for your products or services. Often marketing campaigns fail because this crucial step was not taken prior to implementing marketing strategies. Even setting up a website without doing this step is a waste of your time and money.

Do It Now!

The very first step in your marketing strategy is to do your research right away so that you get started properly.

Identify the buyers of your products and services. What problems do your products and services solve for them?

The 4 Quadrants of Online Business

When it comes to identifying your ideal customer, it is necessary to analyze the four quadrants of business. Even though this may seem advanced, this will help you determine which types of clients you should focus on attracting. The four quadrants of business are based on the combination of two factors:

- Customer Value: How much is a client worth? If a client is worth little to your bottom line, you need to spend less time trying to attract him or her. More time and energy should be devoted to attracting those who make sizeable purchases.

- Search Volume: Are there lots of people searching for the product or service you are offering? If you have multiple services or products in your business, concentrate your marketing strategies on the ones for which more people are searching.

When it comes to Internet marketing, the four quadrants of business are:

1. Low customer value, low search volume: a poor choice to target.

2. Low customer value, high search volume: better, but not great.

3. High customer value, low search volume: even better but not ideal.

4. High customer value, high search volume: the best.

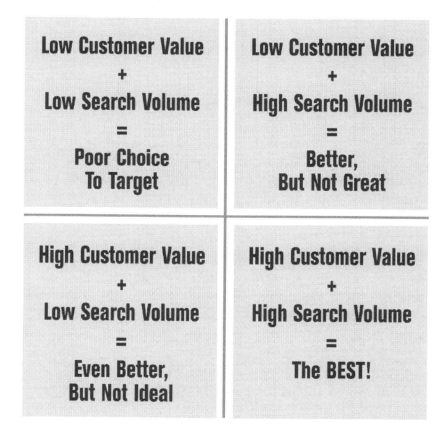

If you pinpoint the customers who have high customer value and high search volume, you can feel confident that those people are very good ones to target. Make sure they also have buying intent, which is also very important.

While all customers are valuable, the others who are not high customer value and high search volume will likely come across your business as you are advertising to that target group. Marketing specifically to the group that has the most potential simply makes good business sense.

Doing Detailed Research

Hand-in-hand with the whole process of identifying your ideal customer is doing detailed research. Even if you know who your ideal customers are but have no idea how to lead them to your site, you will not be successful in converting them to actual customers. This is typically a one-time task done at the beginning of your online marketing campaign and can be delegated to an online research specialist for extremely effective results.

The Necessity of Good Research

Good research online means keyword and key-phrase research. Keyword research is like turning on the light. By doing keyword research, you will know, and not guess, exactly what your potential customers are searching for when they look for services and products like you offer. Simply knowing who your ideal customers are is not enough. You have to know the phrasing they use when they search. When you discover those phrases, your keyword research is done.

Luckily, the keyword research portion of the marketing plan only needs to be done once unless you diversify the line of products or services you offer, new uses are discovered for them, or you open a new division of your company.

In order to nail down the keywords that are being used to find companies in your field, ask yourself some questions.

How Will People Search for You?

What types of phrasing will potential customers use when searching for you? Will they look for a person, position, a firm or a solution? Will they use geographic modifiers like a city, state or region? Will their level of motivation come through in their search by using specific words? Here are various examples of the ways in which people conduct online searches to find what they're looking for:

- Specific Person:
  - o Plumber
  - o Plumbing contractor

- Geographic Modifiers:
  - o Plumber Chicago
  - o Plumber Chicago, IL

- Motivation Levels:
  - o Emergency plumber Chicago
  - o 24-hour plumber

As a critical part of your keyword research, you should employ a keyword research tool. With the death of Google's free Keyword Tool (External) and the current functionality of Google's new Keyword Planner, you'll have to rely on the variety of commercial keyword tools on the market to help you get specific data on the keywords and phrases for your business. These tools can help you greatly, as they can generate keyword ideas for you, as well as synonyms and cross-reference your keywords with geographic modifiers. This will often help you be as effective as possible in getting ranked according to strong keywords. The more precise the keyword, the better conversion rate it will have for sales.

Tools To Make It Easier

Use Market Samurai (http://www.MarketSamurai.com, as of this writing they have a free trial of their keyword software) or another pay site for further building a list of long-tail keywords. They can help you determine which very specific keywords are most valuable. It will also give you an inside look at which words your competitors are using and the quality of the SEO competition they present, when you do a keyword search for them.

Document Data for Future Use

Be sure to keep a running tab of all the keywords you discover. This will give you information to work with for your online content. It will also keep you from having to repeat the keyword search.

Keywords will be used in every aspect of your online marketing. For this reason, the research you do in the beginning about your ideal customer and how they search will carry over to all of your online content. You will use those keywords for:

- Articles
- Blogs
- Search engine optimization
- Press releases
- Mobile site
- Ads
- Social media
- Videos and audios
- Tags

Even simply adding one or more traffic methods per month to your existing traffic generating strategies will produce significant results. Target a couple more keywords from your keyword list each month.

Do Website Optimization Updates

Website optimization is sometimes called onsite search engine optimization. This one-time activity will transform your website from whatever it is presently to a search engine optimized version that is much more attractive to web crawlers. This is extremely important in getting your website ranked as high as possible in the search engine results. The things that are appealing to a search engine are not the same as those things that are esthetically pleasing on a website. In many cases, such fancy programming on a site is a negative for search engines.

Analyze What You Have

First you will need to begin by analyzing your current site, so look at these things:

- Consider the look and feel of the site.

- Is the site optimized for visitors?

- Is the site optimized for search engines?

- Does the site work for multiple browsers?

Critical Components of a Good Website

In most cases, websites are lacking in some of these areas. In order to make your website appealing to human visitors and search engines and be effective in its purposes, you will need to go through and make sure certain things are in place. If they are not, you need to include the following for the best results possible:

- Easy navigation: Make sure the site is easy to use and straightforward.

- Most important information "above the fold": Make sure all the important information is visible when a visitor first arrives at the home page. A good number of people will not scroll down to find the important information.

- All links are correctly working: Don't frustrate visitors or the search engines with broken links.

- Homepage, products page, services page, testimonials, about, and contact form.

- Directed navigation through the site: Make sure you are taking visitors exactly where you want them to go on your site.

- Specific instructions.

- Multiple calls to action: Such as call now, buy now, etc.

- Pictures used correctly: This includes proper sizing of pictures as well as using captions to explain what the pictures represent.

- Non-distracting design: This goes for a background that is too distracting as well as crazy fonts, italics, and underlines.

- Centered layout that has dark text on a light background.

- Multiple ways to contact: With the phone number on the top right, side and bottom and the address only at the bottom.

- Trust factors: Like BBB and awards clearly displayed on the front page.

- Testimonials and reviews on the front page.

- Personal branding: This includes pictures of you and your staff, branded vehicles, audio and video messages and links to any social networking sites like Facebook or Twitter.

- Optimization for keywords: Using good keywords is huge to search engines, and you must take some time to do keyword research before you can determine if keywords are optimized properly.

- Relevancy: Search engines love websites that show relevancy. This is done by starting broad and then drilling down in themes. Always optimize for one keyword per page instead of multiple keywords per page.

- Ensure keywords are in all title tags, meta tags, the URL and the headers and description of your pages.

- Good content: Guarantee all text on your website is search engine optimized with strategic use of keywords and avoid duplicate content.

- Avoid Flash and frames.

With the onsite SEO updates completed, your website should naturally move closer to the top of search engine results. However, you cannot rely on this alone. You must also continue with your online marketing plan and maintain a blog, do other Web 2.0 applications, keep adding citation around the web, use video, reviews and submit articles with links back to your website to increase traffic and to get quality one-way links to help get to the very top of the results.

Add a Lead Capture System to Your Website

By adding a lead capture system to your website you are taking the destiny of your business into your hands. No longer are you simply a passive participant who casts a line and waits for the fish to come to you.

With a lead capture system, you can get the names and contact information of people who visit your site for any reason. This means that you can now build a database of potential customers and market to them. When you need more business, you market to those people, and you can create cash on demand.

All types of sales are dependent on leads. For this reason, having a lead capture system is a wise move in your online marketing strategy. It gives you something tangible to work with when you need more sales. And who doesn't need more sales?

Lead Capture Systems Defined

A lead capture system is simply an opt-in box that offers more information, an e-newsletter subscription, a free report or some other freebie in exchange for simple contact information. Typically the information requested is just a name and email address, but some systems do ask for a mailing address and a phone number. Try to refrain from requesting too much information.

Because these people have come to your site and then opted to get on your email list, you can feel confident that they are interested in your products or services. This makes them likely customers.

Once the lead capture system is in place on your website, you will need to do lead nurturing. This means you must stay in touch with these people. Here are some ways in which you can maintain contact:

- Send newsletters regularly, but not too frequently.

- Keep them up to date on new offerings and sales.

- Offer special deals for those on your email list. This is a very good way to generate business when things are slow.

As a part of this process, you will need to do some of the things that were mentioned in the "Seven Things No One Is Doing" section.

You will need to put autoresponders in place so that as people opt in, they are greeted, welcomed and introduced to your products or services through a series of letters. If you haven't used a free report to get them to join your email list, offer it now.

By building your email list and marketing to it regularly with useful information, you will get the power of having a bigger customer base and being able to generate cash on demand.

Building an Email List

There are a number of excellent reasons why you should start to build an email list for your business. Large companies recognize the value of email lists, but often small companies do not. However, you should know the many advantages of an email list:

- Multiple selling opportunities. If visitors come to your website and don't buy anything or contact you, once they leave, they may be gone for good. If, however, there is an email list for them to subscribe to, then you will still be able to maintain contact with them and, therefore, have more chances to sell to that visitor.

- Send out special offers, holiday specials, breaking news, new product photos, and case studies, etc.

- More sales to existing customers. Because your existing customers will be on the email list, they will also be in steady contact with you, and this will allow you to give special offers and promotions that will induce further sales.

- More referral opportunities. You can utilize your email list to ask for and probably get more referrals.

- Creates a branding image.

- Positions you as an "authority" if done properly.

By effectively using your email list, you will be on your way to helping your business thrive. Smart businesses recognize the value of successful email lists and see growth in their sales.

Implement Personal Branding Changes

By doing one-time personal branding changes, you can affect the kind of change you want in the results you get from your website. You want your website to have a certain kind of feel to it, so you give the impression to visitors that you are indeed a trusted expert in your local market. By tapping into the unique resources the Internet offers, you can help do that and increase traffic and buying customers at the same time.

You are trying to appeal to a sophisticated audience. They are savvy to the things marketers throw at them. They research purchases much more than ever before. However, their attention spans are relatively short, and they make decisions quickly. They are not completely at ease doing business online yet and question whether or not they should trust what they find there. When they come across your website, they want to be sure it's the right source for what they are seeking. They want to know about your company, your commitment to service and your trustworthiness.

By putting the right content on your site, you can build your personal brand and reassure your customers that you can offer what they are looking for. You want to personalize the process for new customers. They want to know about you and your business. For this reason, get personal and let them know who they are doing business with.

Stay away from the "stuffy" corporate sounding websites. No one wants to do business with a big company. They want to do business with neighbors they can trust. Some tweaks to your site can give that impression and help increase sales for you.

Some of the things to include on your website to help you create this personal touch include:

- Photographs and information about the owner and staff

- Expert articles you've written

- Reviews

- Awards

- Professional associations

- Business groups you are a member of
- References from other businesses
- Audio or video messages from the owner
- Audio or video testimonials from customers

You and your business need to be perceived as friendly, not stuffy. By taking the time to invest in personal branding, you will attract more and more buying customers. You will be gaining the trust needed to succeed in the online marketplace.

CHAPTER 6

Tasks that Repeat

Once you have completed the one-time tasks for your local business online marketing plan, you will need to start on the tasks that repeat. These will need to become a regular part of your routine. While some of the repeated tasks are only done every month or even less often, others need to be done daily or a couple of times each week.

The tasks that you will need to repeatedly do in order to build-up your online presence and drive as much traffic as possible to your traffic include:

- Article marketing
- Press releases
- Video marketing
- Reputation Marketing
- SMS/Text Marketing
- Local SEO
- Natural SEO
- Mobile Marketing
- Pay-per-click campaigns
- Report generation
- Testing/tracking
- Blogging
- Directory submission
- Adding testimonials
- Web 2.0.

Dealing with Tasks that Repeat

You can choose to take on these tasks yourself, delegate them to someone who works for you or subcontract them to a third party who specializes in such areas. If you hire a specialist, you can have them take on all of the above tasks or just select ones. Most Internet Marketing Partners who specialize in online marketing give you an à la carte option or a package covering all your online marketing needs.

Scheduling the Tasks that Repeat

If you choose to do the online marketing tasks that repeat yourself, you will need to learn strategies for each and plan them into your work week. Regularity with such tasks is vitally important to the success of your marketing plan. For this reason, a good idea is to add your repeated tasks to your calendar/planner so they are done with the frequency that is necessary.

Article Marketing

Article marketing is simply the writing of approximately 500-word articles on a subject that is somehow related to your business or industry. These content-rich articles are then published online through a variety of article submission sites. The resource box typically found at the bottom of the article is how readers find your company information and are directed to your website. Article marketing is so simple that many people overlook its power and effectiveness.

The Importance of Article Marketing

Article marketing is one of the absolute best ways to put Internet marketing to work for your business. By strategically writing articles that are relevant to your industry and submitting them to online article submission sites you will create a direct path to your website for anyone who does a search for information that relates to your business.

Remember that an article is not a sales pitch. It needs to be full of relevant information that is useful and entertaining. It must also be written using search engine optimization techniques. Be careful not to keyword stuff your articles. Never plagiarize content from anywhere else.

Once you write good articles that teach your customers something while establishing yourself as a go-to expert in the industry, you will need to get the articles published in a variety of places. EzineArticles.com and Squidoo are two excellent locations for publishing such articles, but ideally you will want to submit your articles to hundreds of websites. Article submission sites can help you do that. Be sure to avoid using duplicate content from your website as this may affect the ranking of your article and your site.

Articles are vital to your Internet marketing plan. For this reason, you will need to produce them regularly. This is where those seeking your keywords will stumble across your company, thanks to the resource box that is always included at the end of your articles. However, they have to get to the bottom of the page to get that information. That means you had better have a captivating article written to keep their attention!

Regular article publication will set you apart from many of your competitors, but you must be consistent. You must create multiple articles each month in order to keep traffic flowing to your site. Luckily, this is a very easy task to subcontract out.

Articles are meant to attract people to your site. They are published on other websites with quality backlinks and citations to your site which creates a bonus for you. As discussed before, the more quality backlinks and citation there are to your site the better.

Use Articles to Create Interest and Reach All Potential Customers

To pique the interest of a wide variety of different possible customers, you will need to write a variety of articles, targeting a variety of subjects. Make sure you write articles that touch on every use of your product or service. Some great article ideas are listed below:

- Tips on the use of your product

- Reasons why someone would want to use your service

- Unconventional uses for your product or service

- Frequently asked questions

- Individual products and services
- How to choose the best provider of your type or service or product
- Things to consider when purchasing
- The advantages of using your product or service
- The disadvantages of not using your product or service
- "How to" articles
- Things you shouldn't do
- Evaluations of different options
- Steps for using your products or services
- How your products or services help people
- Little known facts
- Explanations
- How to avoid a problem
- Tips on responding to a challenge

Once you have chosen a subject for an article, it should be in the 400-750 word range. Make sure the article is well-written and flows naturally to keep people reading. Nothing turns a reader off faster than poor grammar and confusing sentences.

The simple formula for article writing as an online marketing technique is as follows:

- Do your keyword research.
- Get your content written.
- Submit it to article directories.

Press Releases

Online press releases are a huge part of building online traffic to your site. They are a credible way to build your online presence. Created to meet strict guidelines, they give select information in a standardized format. Press releases published on certain online press release distribution sites can be picked up and republished in other places. This greatly helps in the increase of traffic to your website through valuable backlinks.

You can create press releases for your business for a wide variety of reasons:

- The launch of a new product, service or line
- Hiring a new professional employee
- Creation of a new division
- Receiving an award
- Milestones in the life of a company
- Reorganization of a company
- Sales related to holidays
- Stock sales
- Partnerships
- Environmentally friendly steps the company is taking
- Contests
- Promotional programs
- New or improved website
- Expert opinions on subjects related to your industry
- Involvement in social causes
- Event involvement

Press releases build even more credibility for your company, as there are more stringent guidelines for the publication of press releases than there are for article publication. If your press release does not comply with the required format and content guidelines, it will not get published. For this reason, many readers will take the information shared in a press release even more seriously than articles or blogs.

Press releases will help get people talking about your business. It will also get you noticed by the search engines, so be sure to create a search engine optimized press release to increase its appeal to web crawlers. When you post it on sites that allow backlinks, press releases can also help direct traffic to your site. The call to action in your press release, such as an offer of more information, should always generate traffic.

Press releases need not be done as often as blogs or articles. However, you should strive to distribute at least one each month. This will set your business apart from the many competitors who do not do it.

Video Marketing

Video marketing is the hot thing in online marketing right now. It appeals to the kind of people who prefer watching videos to gain information rather than reading about it. In a culture that grew up on television, video marketing is an ideal way to get the message across. It can also be much more cost-effective than using TV advertising, which is too costly for the majority of local businesses and is a much less targeted form of marketing.

Video marketing offers a variety of creative options, including the option of teaching with slides of information being shown while a narrator speaks; pictures that give a great visual being presented to music; or an actual video clip that has been produced. In fact, you can even do a combination of these types.

Video marketing allows you to do the following:

- Give a tour of your facilities.

- Provide demonstrations.

- Instruct on the use of your products.

- Solving common problems.

- Provide amazing before and after samples for services.

- Present webinars.

- Share testimonials.

- Show company overviews.

- Share expert articles.

- Deal with questions.

- Present the company owner in an interview.

There are endless uses for video marketing. Because of the visual interest factor, it is useful both onsite and offsite to meet a variety of marketing needs:

- Use to grab the attention of visitors and have them "stick around" your site.

- Many lazy visitors would rather watch a short video than read a bunch of text.

- Use it to brand yourself.

- Use it to build trust.

- Use it to inform or educate visitors.

- Use it offsite to grab searchers and redirect them to your site or phone number.

- Use it to get rankings for multiple keywords or rankings in suburbs of major metropolitan areas.

- Use it to spice up external landing pages and Web 2.0 properties.

- Get your business in multiple places.

Creating quality video is not a complicated process, but it does require time and some knowledge.

SMS/Text Message Marketing

The next wave of local marketing strategy your business needs to jump on is SMS/Text Message Marketing. Quickly becoming recognized as a mass media channel, marketing to your customers on their mobile devices via text message is now one of the most powerful ways to reach them.

SMS / Text marketing is not a strategy you can just jump in and do, however. Just like any other form of advertising, if it's done poorly, you'll only succeed in irritating your prospective and current customers. If it's done well, you may be astounded by the results.

Currently, one reason SMS/Text Message Marketing is so effective is that the 'open rate' for text messages is nearly 100%. It would be nearly impossible to reach a success rate approaching anywhere near that figure with email marketing or direct mail.

SMS / Text marketing can effectively accomplish these tasks for your business:

- Increase brand awareness.

- Gather customer information for marketing purposes.

- Draw customers into buying mode more consistently.

Here are some SMS/Text marketing tactics businesses are seeing success with now:

- Polls

- Trivia contests and sweepstakes

- Instant win games

- Free giveaways

- Alerts about sales and other deals

- Graphics and other messages that are so engaging they get forwarded to your customers' contacts

SMS / Text Message Marketing strategies, like online marketing, are constantly evolving. If you begin an SMS / Text message marketing campaign, be sure that you learn, stay on top of, and follow the rules of the game, so you don't inadvertently cause problems for your business.

Local SEO and Natural SEO

Search engine optimization or SEO, is vital to the implementation of your online marketing plan. While this is a part of the five one-time things you must do to get your plan started successfully, it must also be monitored and updated, so that your local business results and your natural search results remain ranked near or at the top.

Local Business Results

Local business results will impact not only the traffic to your website, but also the phone at your place of business. Since your phone number is listed in the local business results, you will find that your phone will ring much more often once your business is successfully located at the top of these results.

Submit your business to the three major local business results sites. Monitor and update listings regularly to secure top spots. Make sure that your listings are search engine optimized. The three sites you must be on are:

- Google
  - This is the most important one as it owns 2/3 of online traffic; your Google My Business listing is especially vital to your success.

- Yahoo
  - This website is also very important.

- Bing
  - This one is growing in importance, but not as prominent as Google and Yahoo

These local business results each pick up on select keywords and use different location modifiers when ranking listings. However, most listings include address, phone number, directions to your physical address, website and customer reviews. The ones with the best reviews containing targeted keywords, in addition to location modifiers, will find their way to the top of the search results.

In order to be listed in the top 10 search results, follow these seven tips:

1. Optimize every aspect of your listing with strategic keywords.

2. Get reviews from customers.

3. Obtain quality backlinks from local online directories.

4. Strategically choose the areas you want to be optimized, even establishing different addresses and phone numbers for other areas.

5. Get listed in about four to five categories related to your business for your business results listing.

6. Place coupons with the listing to increase conversion rates.

7. Use YouTube Videos and photographs with your keyword in the title.

After listing in the top local business results, seek out other directory listings to use such as Kudzu, City Search, cmac.ws, Best of the Web local and more.

Track the changes you make, so that you can keep the listing as relevant and consistent as possible. It will also help you monitor what works and what doesn't. Be patient, it sometimes takes three to four weeks to see your listing appear.

Natural Results

Natural results are not paid for and are also referred to as organic results as they are generated by the search engines themselves. Typically placed below local searches with the map and paid searches, many people consider them the most valid type of search results.

It is possible to get a variety of listings in the natural results. Anything that has relevant content on it, especially if it has been search engine optimized, can be included in natural results. Search engine rankings can include:

• Your main website

- Social media content

- Articles

- Press releases

- Other Web2.0 content

- Landing pages

- Videos

- Social bookmarks

- Directory listings

- Blog posts

Keyword research is vital to the successful ranking of your website and other content in the natural results of search engines. For this reason this step is not to be overlooked. The relevancy of your content is very important to the placement. Other ranking factors that impact where your content will show up in ranking results include:

- Content congruency/consistency

- Keywords used in page links

- Keywords in the content

- Citations

- Google Page Rank

- Quality Backlinks - Links pointing back to your site/content

In fact, good relevant content with keywords, lots of good citations and enough quality backlinks will be sure to make it to the top of many categories within a given period. Get citations and links to your site from local directories, authority sites, article marketing, Web 2.0, blogs, social bookmarks and video marketing. The more quality citations and backlinks you have to your site, the more successful it will be in ranking.

Mobile Marketing

The newest player on the local marketing strategy scene is mobile marketing. We're becoming a multi-screen 24/7 society using smartphones, tablets, laptops and computers on a daily basis. And now with more searches being done on mobile devices than traditional computers, Mobile Marketing is quickly becoming recognized as the new SEO. As this trend continues to grow, having your customers find you on mobile friendly websites is more critical than ever. Your business needs to have a mobile marketing presence, PERIOD! Why? Because marketing to your customers on their mobile devices is now one of the most powerful ways to reach them.

So what's the first step? Create the hub of your Mobile Marketing system, a well designed Mobile Website.

What is a mobile website?

According to Wikipedia, it's *"the use of browser-based Internet services, from a handheld mobile device, such as a smartphone, a feature phone, or a tablet computer, connected to a mobile network or other wireless network."*

In short, a mobile website is an app that allows online websites to be viewed on mobile devices – anytime, anywhere.

Mobile marketing is not only here to stay, it's growing rapidly and becoming a major piece of your online marketing plan. In fact, 1 in 5 searches has local intent, and here are the results of these local searches:

- 94% of smartphone users search for location information

- 51% visited the business

- 48% called the business

- 29% made a purchase at the business and did so quickly

- 80% of mobile search triggered store visits happen within 5 hours of the initial search

- 85% of mobile search triggered calls to stores happen within 5 hours of the initial search

Here is what Google has to say about people's experiences on mobile:

"57% of users say they won't recommend a business with a poorly designed mobile site, and 40% have turned to a competitor's site after a bad mobile experience."

So the importance of not just having a mobile website, but a well-designed mobile website creating a great mobile experience is critical to your success and bringing in more customers online. There are two prevalent types of Mobile Websites:

- Responsive Site – Your desktop website coded to adjust to mobile devices.

- Mobile Optimized Site – Built on a separate platform for mobile traffic.

Though responsive sites at first glance sound like a great idea, many are very slow to load on mobile devices and can lead to a poor mobile experience. On the other hand, a mobile optimized website, built on a mobile platform for speed, easy navigation and a great mobile experience is the best way to go. A good mobile website platform will also have many tools built in to make your mobile site shine, such as analytics, loyalty programs, lead capture systems and more.

The Keys to a Good Mobile Website and marketing campaign:

- Easy Navigation

- Tap to call

- Map – click for directions

- Links to your social media

- Links to leave reviews

- Loyalty program

- Information that a mobile minded visitor would find helpful

Your mobile website design is going to be very different than your desktop site not just because the size of the screen, but because of the mindset of and needs of the mobile user.

You will need to identify what your mobile consumers need the most when they interact with your business on mobile and put the focus on your value proposition and how it relates to a mobile-centric user.

As you can see, having a mobile website isn't just a good suggestion for business owners today; it's a **must** unless your goal is to lose customers by the day. Nearly all business owners have realized by this point just how important the Internet is to their business, and many have already gone to great lengths to promote the blogs on their website and take full advantage of SEO opportunities, and in many cases, even build a full e-commerce website. And while that main website is a huge source of revenue, there's another website that you could be missing, and that is becoming even more important than your main website.

Mobile marketing strategies, just like online marketing, are constantly evolving. When you begin a mobile marketing campaign, be sure that you learn, stay on top of, and follow the rules of the game, so you don't inadvertently cause problems for your business.

Pay-Per-Click Advertising

Pay-per-click campaigns and advertising are one area where many people are already investing in online marketing. You may be one of those who recognize the value of such campaigns in finding potential customers. One of the major advantages of PPC campaigns is the fact that you can be up and running with traffic actually coming to your website in as little as one day.

Pay-per-click campaigns can also be very expensive. However, they can be greatly downsized and often even completely eliminated by the effective use of an online marketing strategy. You can easily spend a lot less on your PPC campaign than you have previously if your business is consistently at the top of search engine results. However, PPC campaigns are still important tools that can remain as a part of a good online marketing strategy, especially for extremely competitive keyword searches.

The Right Keyword Research

Keyword research will be the thing that makes your PPC campaigns work like never before. If you have your keyword research done correctly, you will have a list of keywords that are used when people search for something your business could provide, including very specific long-tail keywords. These keywords will not only be the ones most commonly used, but also the ones that have the fewest PPC matches for them. This means when someone uses those keywords your ad will appear at the top, not mixed in somewhere with endless others.

Keyword research makes all the difference between hit or miss PPC campaigns and ones that work and have a high rate of conversions to sales for the number of click-throughs that you get. Having professional management of your PPC campaigns can mean huge savings and much greater results.

Geo-Targeting Your Ads

Most people are not familiar with this type of PPC option. However, it allows you to target your PPC ads to just the people in your area who are searching for a given term. Using geo-targeting, a search by someone in your geographic area for a generic term like "plumber" would reveal your ad, whereas someone in another state or area that you don't serve who searches for "plumber" would not see your ad.

Using Google Adwords and other PPC services, such as Facebook, Gmail & LinkedIn, you can choose to have your ads shown only to people living in certain zip codes, cities or regions. By doing so, you can bid on very generic terms that previously would not have been a good choice. This is possible because search engines know where searchers are located. You can choose to target:

- Actual location

- Narrow geography such as city, state or metro area

- IP address

In addition, you can choose to do PPC campaigns on words with a location qualifier attached to them. Many people will choose to include the location qualifier in their search, such as "Milwaukee plumber." By using both the searcher's actual location and where the searcher is looking, you will have the greatest success possible in your pay-per-click campaign.

The advantages to geo-targeting generic terms for your PPC ads are:

- Cheaper click rates
- Fast traffic results
- More targeted traffic
- Lower competition
- Higher conversion to sales

The Importance of the Landing Page

A landing page is the page a prospect reaches when they click on your ad, on a link in your article's resource box, or on a link in a press release, video, or audio. The best-designed landing pages have a way these visitors can trade their contact information for a special report or some other content that's valuable to them. The landing page is a very important component of the online marketing strategy for pay-per-click campaigns. It should be relevant to the ad that you have placed and should contain keywords related to the search. You should have a different landing page for each PPC ad you place. Include navigation links to other parts of your website for even better results on Google.

Consider Using a Content Network PPC Campaign

Content network PPC allows you to sell advertising space on your website and use the space on other websites that relate to yours. What's most effective about advertising with the content network is the fact that most of the time people spend online isn't spent using a search engine, but visiting their favorite sites. Content PPC allows you to get your ad in front of them while they're on these popular sites.

A large number of websites collaborate in a content network, and you get the advantage of the traffic attracted to each of them. Your ad can be so much more than a text ad like traditional PPC. You can opt for images and even video to capture the attention of potential customers. Content network PPC is wide open right now and is an excellent option to explore in your online business plan.

Blogging

Blogging can be one of the most effective ways to get yourself to the top of the search engine results for your chosen keywords. Google and other search engines regularly visit blogs and re-index the content found there because they love such applications. For this reason, if you regularly blog, your site will get increasingly better results on search engines. As more and more backlinks are built, the traffic to your site will increase.

Shorter than an article, with fewer guidelines than a press release, blogs can be quick and easy to produce. However, they must also meet SEO criteria for maximum effectiveness. This means you should focus on keywords, specifically long-tail keywords, when you blog. However, be sure not to "stuff" keywords into the text. It should have a natural flow, so people keep coming back to it, want to read it and subscribe to your RSS feed.

Below are some tips for blogging:

- Keep blog posts short – under 400 words.

- Use keywords in the title and throughout the blog.

- Add an image for visual interest.

- Schedule the appearance of a new blog about every three days or even more often depending on the industry..

- Make blog posts relevant to what is happening in the news.

- Don't use a blog to rant about something. Keep it informative.

You can also use offsite blogs to increase traffic to your website by using Web 2.0 and offsite blogs such as:

- **Squidoo.com**

- **WordPress.com**

- **HubPages.com**

- **Tumblr.com**

- **Blogger.com**
- **Quora.com**
- **Zimbio.com**
- **Postach.io**
- **Medium.com**
- **Svbtle.com**
- **Xanga.com**
- **LiveJournal.com**

Create even more quality backlinks by submitting your offsite blog posts to social networking and social news sharing sites.

The Importance of Blog Comments

Your blog is essentially a forum for others to interact with you. Those who make comments are likely to be potential customers or even existing customers. Always respond to valid questions, comments and complaints. The way in which you handle such things will speak volumes to the followers of your blog.

Bear in mind that you can learn a lot from the comments your blog receives. Your next big product or service is often waiting to be discovered in the feedback from a customer or potential customer. They may share with you what little thing bothers them most or what would be an ideal addition to what you offer. This interaction that allows you to garner knowledge from those who buy from you is one of the most important aspects of a blog. Use it!

You should also take the time to comment on other blogs related to your field and leave your website address to create more valuable backlinks. Do not make a comment that is little more than an ad for your own business. It will likely not even be approved if you attempt to do so. Make relevant, helpful comments. Leave your website URL in the space provided only.

Directory Submission

Links are the key to getting listed high in search engine results. One-way links are what you want, so make sure you focus on getting your site listed in as many places as possible. Directory submissions are excellent ways to get your site's link out there, even though many people will tell you that business directories are outdated. They do indeed have great value in getting backlinks to your website.

The types of directories you should submit to include:

- Major directories, like the fee-based Yahoo directory and the free human-reviewed DMOZ

- Local directories, like local.com, localeze.com, hotfrog.com and specific group directories like your local chamber of commerce

- Industry specific and niche directories, such as cmac.ws and other niche groups found through online searches

- Yellow Pages/411 directories like YellowPages.com, Superpages.com, Yellowbook.com, InfoUSA.com and Localeze.com

- Review directories like Kudzu.com, Insiderpages.com, Tripadvisor.com, AngiesList.com, BBB.org and Citysearch.com

These directories will help customers and potential customers locate your business much easier. Your business will typically be at or near the top of search results for a business name or the niche and location. For this reason, your presence in the relevant directories will get you near the top of results. Your website traffic and your phone inquiries will increase as a result of being listed in directories. For that reason, directory submissions are a solid part of any marketing plan.

Inclusion in directories will also validate a company's existence for search engines. It creates backlinks to the website, and citations that help the search engines index a company. Newer directories with Web 2.0 capabilities even have the interactive option of adding reviews, which creates even more content for a site. This means better natural search results and local search results for your business.

Most directories are free of charge. However some have a fee associated with them. If it is a big-name, powerful directory, it may be worth the investment.

Review directories serve a variety of purposes, such as:

- Quality Backlinks

- Citations

- Reviews

- Local rankings

- Building customer trust

Citations are becoming one of the most important reasons to make sure your business is included in review directories. Essentially a citation is a third-party endorsement of your business. It acts as a vote of confidence Google can lean on in including your business at the top of Google My Business Pages results. Citations create credibility for your site in the eyes of the search engines. The more citations your business has, linking from other reputable sites, the better.

The Validity Testimonials Create

Testimonials are an excellent way to build consumer confidence in your products or services. Visitors to your site are witness to actual customers and their level of satisfaction with your company. They see how your products are put to use and also get ideas as to how they can use them.

You can add video testimonials for maximum impact, as they appeal to everyone, even those who typically don't take the time to read websites, and create a type of social proof that helps your personal branding. Alternatively you can post a testimonial in text form with accompanying pictures of the client and even the client using your company's services or products. You can also use simple audio clips for testimonials.

Some tips for the use of testimonials:

- Get testimonials from both genders.

- If your product or service is used in a variety of different ways or industries, get testimonials from various areas.

- Put some diversity of age and ethnicity in your testimonials.

- Feel free to use just a portion of a testimonial if it is too lengthy.

- Ask customers for testimonials that you can use.

New customers feel more confident about their decision to purchase from you if you have testimonials on your site. They get the impression that they are a part of a group and are not just another sale.

In every testimonial you must include:

- Customer's name and title

- City and state

- Credentials

Encourage them to talk about the way your business helped to solve their problem. Always get permission from the person to use the testimonial and information in it before publishing it. Keep a copy of the permission for reference.

Reputation Marketing

Did you notice I didn't say reputation management, a term you've probably heard a lot? The reason is that reputation management is obsolete. The truth is when was the last time you made any revenue managing? You haven't. Management is a company expense. You generate revenue marketing. And this entire book is about you getting more business online and increasing your revenues and ROI.

Social Proof: Reviews are the New Gold Standard

While it's true that testimonials on your website are important to build consumer confidence, reviews and recommendations on social media and review sites are becoming the gold standard. That's because they're considered independent, so they're more trustworthy and carry a heavier weight with Google and in your customer's minds. These reviews are being left directly by the clients and consumers on these sites and are seen almost everywhere.

And even though this is a relatively new aspect of your online business plan, over the next 2 years you'll see reviews and online reputation become the dominate factor as to why some businesses soar to success and others fail miserably with their online marketing. That's a pretty bold statement, and you may be asking yourself, why do I say this? Very simply, because everyone reads and relates to reviews.

Think about the last time you purchased something on Amazon, eBay or any other online store. Did you read some or all of the reviews about the product, service and seller? Did it affect your decision-making process? Of course, it did. It's human nature to see what others say and seek the approval of society, peers, colleagues, etc.

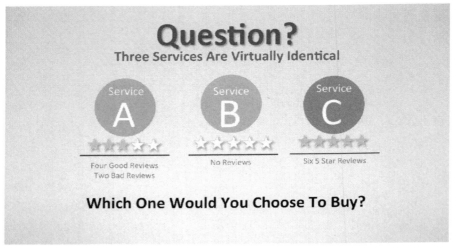

"These five stars are like a huge billboard saying, I'm the right company for you to choose."

The same is true of local and service based businesses. People read reviews and use those reviews to weight out with which businesses they will do business. And this fact has become even more profound because of all the changes Google has made.

You see, very recently, Google merged 80 million Google+ Pages with each company's websites listings with their reviews listed right on the website. This now shows up in every Google search.

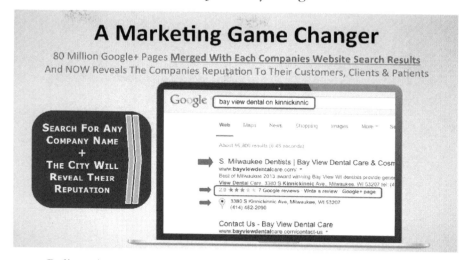

Believe it or not, you can search for any company name plus the city, and it reveals their reputation. As you can see in the above screenshot, Gentle Dental Jefferson Ave. If I go to Google and just type in Gentle Dental Jefferson Ave, you can see the first line is always the company website. The next two lines are a little bit about that company, and the third line is their reputation. They have a 2.5 star reputation. You can see that Google has indexed their Google+ page and merged it with their website listing.

I'd like for you to see this for yourself. Stop reading right now and go to your computer or smartphone and take a look at your online reputation. Go to Google.com and type in your company name and city and see what people are finding out right now about you when they search.

Reviews show up not only on Google but:

- Google My Business Maps listing

- Pay Per Click (PPC)

- Social Media like Facebook and LinkedIn

- Local directories like Yelp and Yellow Pages

- Website rankings
- Organic rankings

"Most people don't know that Facebook is now the number two mobile app for searching for businesses online."

Customer reviews are now a major factor in reputation because they now show up virtually everywhere online.

Your Online Reputation is More Critical Than Ever

Why Reputation is Vital to any Business:

- 72% of Buyers trust reviews as much as personal recommendations
- Consumers Look up an average of 10 reviews before making a decision
- 70% of Consumers Trust a Business with a Minimum of 6-10 reviews
- Without Six 5-Star Reviews, your business isn't trusted
- Positive Yelp ratings can boost a restaurant's nightly reservations by 19%

How would a 19% monthly increase to your business affect your bottom line?

Here's some more food for thought…

- Existing customers who look up your phone number to call or directions to your location, they are going to see your online reputation score.
- Reviews send you prequalified, presold customers because buyers trust reviews as much as personal recommendations

"Reputation Marketing Has Proven to Increase business by 19% by increasing ½ Star Rating Online."

3 Steps to position you and your business as a market leader.

Step 1 - Track Your Reputation: Monitor what are people saying about you.

Most of your competitors, if they do anything, will do this with some cheap reporting service and think they are getting the job done and stop there. This couldn't be further from the truth. Not only is this a defensive posture, the truth is waiting to see what people say, and reacting to those reviews isn't going to bring in more customers into your business. Think about it. Do you make money managing or marketing? Of course, marketing. So while this is an important step, it's only the first step in your reputation marketing plan.

Step 2 - Build Your Reputation

This is where you begin to become proactive in your online reputation, building a culture within your business from employees to the CEO, how to ask for reviews, utilize surveys, and get feedback from your customers and clients regarding all aspects of your business.

Step 3 - Marketing Your Reputation.

This is when it gets fun and where you are positioning yourself and your business as an authority in your market and industry and as a market leader online via your website, social media, online images and videos. By using image reviews, video reviews, and review commercials, you maximize your impact online by tapping into the way people like to communicate the most, visually.

Web 2.0 Marketing

The importance of Web 2.0 Marketing can't be stressed enough. Web 2.0 is a term used to refer to any applications that allow users to interact. Social networks, blogs, video sharing sites, wikis and more are some of the commonly used Web 2.0 applications that can be used as an effective part of any online marketing campaign. In fact, many of these types of applications allow an excellent source for feedback to a company.

One of the major purposes of using Web 2.0 in your quest to drive traffic to your website is to create quality backlinks to your site. So you will need to make comments on other sites with links back to your own sites. You will also need to create your own blog posts, videos and social network identities to share useful information for those who would be potential customers for you.

As with any of the online writing you do, pay close attention to make sure that it's search engine optimized. Use keywords strategically in your content. This will ensure that you get the best ranking possible in relevant searches.

By using Web 2.0, you are opening up your business to explosive growth. It's easy for fans of your service to share it with others.

The feedback you receive from Web 2.0 gives you a wealth of opportunities:

- As individuals leave testimonials, you build credibility.

- As customers leave comments and suggestions, you get important feedback that allows you to tweak your product to serve your customers best. You will be much more on target with their needs.

- As complaints are dealt with, your reputation for customer service is built.

Right now, Google, the leading search engine worldwide, loves Web 2.0 content such as:

- Videos

- Press releases

- Articles

Therefore, careful use of search engine optimized content on such sites will help give you the ranking you want on the search engines.

Social Media and Social Networking

Web 2.0 applications must be updated very regularly. Among your arsenal of tools in this category should definitely be Facebook, LinkedIn, Google+ and Twitter. These are very important online marketing tools for most businesses which have a strong online presence. However, they must regularly be updated, preferably daily. This makes it a very daunting task for anyone who is short on time or is not a fan of social networking.

Think of Facebook as an extension of your email list. More and more people are shying away from communicating through email and are instead using Facebook. You can create an account that lets customers and potential customers friend you and like your business page.

As you build your network of friends and fans, be sure to regularly post specials, information about products and services and more. Status updates should be used to share brief tidbits of information similar to an abbreviated version of a newsletter or special announcement that you would make through your email list. As friends and fans interact with you and leave comments be sure to answer their messages. This will help you develop a relationship, which is becoming more and more important to people in their choice of who they do business with.

You should also take the time to "Like" other businesses that are complementary to yours. A comment you make on a status they put up could be seen by countless potential new customers.

Twitter is like a mini-Facebook with only short Tweets allowed instead of long-winded status updates. You can follow others who Tweet and build a following of your own. Twitter is instantaneous and reaction to anything you put there can be very fast.

Among the social media sites that you should interact with are:

- Facebook
- Twitter
- YouTube
- LinkedIn

- Google +

- Pinterest

- Google Profiles

- Social bookmarking sites

Additional Traffic Strategies

By using a wide variety of traffic strategies, you will have the best chance of being able to attract the maximum number of potential customers to your website. Apart from the techniques already mentioned, there are other ones that will help you drive traffic to your site. Some of them are even completely free while others involve a varying amount of investment depending on the quality of equipment you want to use to create the medium.

Classified Ads

By placing carefully created online classified ads you can easily drive traffic to your website. Many of these websites are free of charge, like Craigslist.org. You can choose to put an ad in the sections that best fit the services or products your company provides. You can even put links directly back to your website in many of these ads. The sheer volume of traffic on such sites will help people find you and your website more readily, as there are numerous people who use such sites as their go-to resource for many things.

To get the maximum amount of use from your classified ads, create links to your ad using social bookmarking sites and other social networking sites. This will create additional backlinks to your ad and help it get ranked on the search engines. Any content that gets ranked on the search engines is excellent for your online marketing.

Make sure the ads you place on classified ad sites are search engine-friendly, like all your online content. Use keywords correctly, without stuffing them into the ad, to maximize your search engine result ranking. Such ads need to be placed monthly to stay current on the search engines. Vary the content though and add seasonal specials, if appropriate.

Some of the best-classified ad sites include:

- Craigslist.org

- Backpage.com

- Topics.com/classifieds/city

- Olx.com

- Oodle.com

- UsFreeAds.com

Local Online Discussion Forums

Make sure you are active in local online discussion forums, as this will help you reach even more potential new customers. Many times people seek out such forums in an attempt to solve a problem they are facing. By being present and taking part in the discussions, you can offer your services to solve appropriate issues. In addition, you will be connecting with potential customers who speak openly about what they can't find or are not being offered. It is a great way to do research in order to fine-tune your offerings to make sure you are actually meeting the needs of those you want to buy from you.

You can find such local forums by doing a simple online search for them. Most require you to create a free account and profile that should include information on your business including a link to your site.

Some tips for optimal use of local online discussion forums as a part of your marketing strategy include:

- Start or contribute to conversations in a relevant way.

- Pay close attention to the forum rules.

- Realize that blatant advertising is a no-no.

- Use an anchor text keyword in your signature.

- Use "how to" articles as good posting content for the forums.

Post weekly or monthly on local online discussion forums to take advantage of the benefits, such as multiple backlinks, that are generated from each post.

Audio Marketing

By doing audio marketing, you can more easily capture the attention of visitors to a site and get them involved in the content you are delivering. In fact, every business owner should incorporate audio marketing both onsite and offsite into their marketing plan. It is much more memorable than text and keeps visitors on a website longer than they would stay otherwise because audio is more of a personable approach.

You can use audio to:

- Introduce your products or services

- Present the owner of the business

- Give consumer tips

- Give instructions

- Present testimonials

- Repurpose radio commercials

- Read blog posts or expert articles

- Give a call to action.

In fact, audio testimonials are a much more effective way of building trust with potential customers.

Offsite audio can be used to drive traffic to your website and to help with the personal branding of your business. It helps the owner appear to be a true expert in the field. Offsite audio also provides quality backlinks to your site and counts as content to help your site's ranking on the search engines.

Opt to put offsite audio on Podcasts, online radio shows or other forms of distribution. You might also want to record a message with expert tips and link it back to your site, to promote yourself as an expert.

Create a title starting with your chosen keyword phrase when you submit your audio to different sites. Use the same keyword in the segment description. You can also drive traffic to your audio content with backlinks, using various online marketing techniques. There are many tools that will help you facilitate the use of audio in your online marketing.

Know Your Numbers

Report Generation, Testing and Tracking

Report generation must regularly be done to stay on top of the performance of your online marketing plan. Through testing and tracking, you can effectively and clearly see what is working and what is not. **So then by doing more of what is working and less of what isn't working, you'll grow faster at less cost.** This is a very important part of your business and must be done at least quarterly unless you are functioning beyond full capacity. As you are implementing or even prior to implementing, take the time to test and track new marketing strategies so that you have a baseline to compare.

Use the following types of data in your analysis of your marketing:

- Rankings
- Links/backlinks
- Traffic sources and volume
- Visitor data
- Visitor actions and behavior

Rankings

You will need to track the main site rankings for your different keywords. This will tell you where each keyword ranks, so you can get an idea of the ranking possibilities for the content you put out there using that keyword. You can use rank checking tools to assist you in tracking rankings for keywords. Check those of your competitors also.

Links/Backlinks

When testing the backlinks of your site, you'll need to find out from where the links are coming. This is to verify that these links are quality backlinks and also a test to make sure that links are working.

Track how many backlinks your site has and how many are recognized by Google. Do the same for your competitors, especially those who already have a good degree of online market domination. This will give you some ideas from where you need to link. You can access link and backlink tracking tools to facilitate the process.

Traffic Sources and Volume

Traffic sources and the volume of traffic need to be tracked and optimized. This will tell you where your visitors are coming from and the number of visitors you are getting from each source. It's important to know if they are direct visitors, referred through natural search engine results, referred from other sites or referred through paid search engine ads. This type of tracking will also reveal the keywords that are working to get visitors to your site. There are traffic tracking tools available for this.

Visitor Data

Visitor data should also be tested, tracked and optimized as a regular part of your marketing program. You want to know where they are located, which web browser they use, the type of operating system they use, connection speed and if they are a brand-new visitor or a repeat one. This will help you create the best visitor experience possible for those who come to your site. The same tracking tools that provide traffic data will also help you track visitor data.

Visitor Actions and Behavior

You will also need to track visitor actions and behavior information. Details like the page of the site the visitor entered on and exited from will divulge the relevant information for which they were looking. With such information, you will learn how well your landing pages and other content are working for you. You can also find out how long they stayed on your site, which will help you come up with ways to keep them there longer.

Record the links that get the most click-through traffic, so that you know what information attracts visitors most. The most important feature of tracking visitor behavior is the fact that you can find out the number of people who took action and what they actually did. There is a variety of technologies that allow you to track such information.

By regularly testing and tracking your site with the collection of important data, you will be equipped to optimize it, so you get the best results possible. You will know what is working well and what needs to be changed. Discern what the data means, so you can change the content or make site adjustments if necessary. This will help you improve your business by getting the right people to your site who will then convert to sales.

Part Three

Online Market Domination Made Easy...

Chapter 7

Stay on Top of Things

By keeping a finger on the pulse of your industry, you will easily find new topics for blogging, articles, press releases, videos, audios and even social networking comments. This way you can quickly jump on new trends as they become popular. Technology can help you do so by staying on top of the latest developments, trends and hot spots in online marketing. You will have a much better chance to keep your online market domination. There are always new developments in the dynamic world of online marketing. Therefore, staying abreast of new technologies and new trends is essential. You can do so by:

- Following Marketing blogs
- Webinars
- Google Hangouts
- Seminars
- Watching the competition
- Subscribing to RSS feeds
- Being on Marketing email lists
- Following experts on Social media

In addition, you can use Google Alerts to stay on top of things happening in the media in either your industry or in a field relevant to yours, as well as in online marketing trends. By setting up a Google Alert, you are automatically informed when information concerning the topics you choose is updated in selected online formats. This helps you to keep on top of things so that you can share relevant information in a timely manner and drive people to your website for relevant solutions.

Are you a Do It Yourselfer or a Delegator?

Online marketing, like any marketing, is multi-faceted and requires a great amount of work and a hefty learning curve for those who have never done it before. Today's marketing requires a lot more maintenance than previously. Even just monitoring your Web 2.0 applications that should be checked daily can eat up precious time in your schedule.

Know Thyself

"Know thyself." The famous words of Socrates rings true for most of life and even more so with your Online Business Plan. The truth is we all have good intentions to grow our businesses and do new things we know we need to do. Implementing your Online Business Plan so that you can dominate your market online is no different. In fact, it is so important that you really need to be brutally honest with yourself and ask, "Am I a DIYer or a Delegator?" Will you take the time needed up front, daily, weekly, monthly and yearly to put these strategies and tactics into play for your business or will another year go by and this time next year you're saying to yourself, "I woulda, coulda, shoulda!" If you know yourself and truly feel you're disciplined enough to take on these tasks, and then by all means do it. **Do It Now**. Finish this book and then register for your free training at DemystifiedBookOnline.com (see back of the book) and implement one thing today in your online business plan. However, if you know deep in your heart you mean well yet you won't follow through with these tasks, then you're a delegator and outsourcing is your best strategy.

It's All about Time

Outsourcing: The Answer to Easy Implementation

By outsourcing your online local marketing, you can ensure that your online marketing is done by those who are skilled in the field. You can conserve your own time to spend on the tasks in your company that rely on you. In addition, the implementation of your marketing changes that are necessary to affect a change in your sales will get done much quicker than if you had to learn how to do it and then do it yourself.

Most business owners are spending 80+ hours weekly in their business, doing the things that are necessary to be successful. These people are masters of their domains and know what they are doing in their field of expertise. However, taking extraordinary amounts of time to learn and master Internet marketing does not always make sense. What does make sense is for them to continue doing the things they know how to do well and let a master in Internet marketing take care of that side of things for them. That is time and resources well spent.

Time is a crucial factor when you think about marketing your business. With the help of a professional Internet marketing strategist, your business could easily rank #1 in Google searches for local keywords in weeks instead of months or years. If you were to do it yourself, where would you be in the process of implementing your online marketing plan? Would you still be learning or procrastinating or would you actually have things done? Do you have the time to devote to this?

Internet marketing strategists can take care of things such as:

- Site design

- Landing pages for PPC campaigns

- Video creation (slide show style)

- Video marketing

- Reputation marketing

- Press release marketing

- Mobile marketing systems

- Directory submissions

- SEO

- Quality backlink generation

- Citation creation

- PPC campaign management

- Social networking setup

- Email marketing setup

- General marketing consulting

The fact is, in each of these categories, there are so many more tasks that must be mastered before implementing them effectively on your website. All aspects can be taken care of quickly and easily by hiring a professional.

Site design:

This can be much more than just creating a site from scratch. Internet marketing strategists can also do any of the following:

- Site cleanup
- SEO Audit
- Meta tag cleanup
- Total redesign
- Set up contact forms
- Add audio
- Add video

Landing pages for PPC:

Internet marketing strategists can help you set up a landing page that:

- Has proper keyword density
- Has an opt-in or capture page for collecting emails to be used later

Content creation:

There is a wide range of services a Internet marketing strategist can handle:

- Website content
- Blog writing
- Article writing
- Email messages
- Free giveaway reports
- Capture page writing

- Press release writing

Video creation:

This can be done in the form of a slide show or even live action. Here they can create videos for:

- Your website
- Capture pages
- Offsite properties
- Video marketing

Video Marketing:

Just what it sounds like, this is marketing with video. This can be done by:

- Submitting to video sharing sites
- Repurposing for multiple keywords and submitting to other sites
- Submitting to external blogs
- Optimizing your video and video channels so your videos are found

Article Writing:

Some Internet marketing strategists and article writing services can:

- Ghostwrite your articles for publication
- Write to submit to article directories
- Position for branding and backlinks

Press Release Marketing:

Some Internet marketing strategists and News Agency services can:

- Write your press release for publication

- Submit your press release to News Agencies
- Rank your press release for important keywords and phrases
- Position you and your company for branding and backlinks

Mobile Websites:

A must for any business who'd like to be found by smartphone users. This is much more than just creating a mobile website. Internet marketing strategists can also do any of the following:

- Build your dedicated mobile website
- Create a great user experience with easy to navigate calls to action
- Track and analyze your mobile visitors for higher ROI
- Build an entire mobile marketing system

Directory Submissions:

This is key for any business and can be done by:

- Submitting to top directories
- Submitting to local directories
- Submitting to niche directories
- Picking a number of directories they will submit your site to each month

Reputation Marketing:

Build trust with customers and search engines by:

- Creating a 5-star reputation
- Having customers, clients and patients leave reviews on social sites, directories and Google+
- Training your staff to get 5-star reviews
- Creating a system which perpetually builds and markets your reviews and reputation

SEO, Quality Backlink Generation and Citation Creation:

Get your website ranked higher in the search engines by:

- Onsite optimization
- Quality backlinks galore
- Pick the number of backlinks you want them to add every month
- Add Citations all across authority sites, directories and social media outlets

PPC Campaign Management:

They manage your PPC campaigns with:

- Google AdWords
- Facebook Ads
- Yahoo Sponsored Search
- Microsoft Ad Center/Bing
- Lesser known PPC spots

Social networking setup:

This is becoming more and more popular these days and with this they can:

- Set up profiles on Twitter, LinkedIn, Google+ and Facebook
- Tweak backgrounds, headers & profile pictures
- Add content
- Create groups
- Add friends, fans, followers. and connections

Email marketing setup:

Internet marketing strategists can help you capture emails and use those emails to:

- Send giveaway reports

- Set up capture pages

- Set up an autoresponder

- Write a series of emails

General marketing consultant:

The sky's the limit here, and Internet marketing strategists can provide:

- Anything that will improve your business

- Guidance and instructions on setting up any of the other business tactics from above

In addition to any or all of these tasks, an Internet marketing strategist can become your online marketing partner, doing all your Internet marketing tasks for you on a constant basis. This makes you essentially competition proof because there is someone staying on top of it all for you and constantly getting more and more links and ranking you for more and more keywords.

Choosing the Right Internet Marketing Partner

If you decide that outsourcing your online marketing out to another firm is the right decision for you, take the time to find the right Internet marketing strategist. You should begin by deciding what you want to be done and what you plan to do yourself. It is fine to let a Internet marketing strategist do it all.

Next find an online marketing strategist who is an authority in the field. Good choices are those individuals who make presentations to business groups on the topic of Internet marketing. Other good choices are those who appear at the top of natural local searches for Internet marketing strategists because that means they can actually do what they say they can do. If an online marketing strategist is everywhere, including in the top several spots in searches, you can feel confident that they are a leader in the field and a good choice for you.

Options in Outsourcing

There are so many different Internet marketing strategists who offer some or all of the things above. Some specialize in just one area while others offer all online marketing services. You need to determine if you want to take care of any of the tasks yourself, with an employee or through a professional. Internet marketing strategists will often provide a variety of options for you to choose from to tailor the service you are purchasing to your needs.

A La Carte:

This is ideal for those who want to keep a hand on things and have a good knowledge of some of the areas of Internet marketing. It also works well for those who want to learn some of the specialties mentioned here.

Package Deals:

The perfect solution for the busy local business person who does not have the time or interest in learning the details of Internet marketing. It allows for quicker implementation of all the different parts of Internet marketing, as there is no learning curve involved. Those who will be doing your marketing already know what they are doing. You just need to prepare for the influx of new business.

Purchasing Leads:

There are companies that have the Internet marketing in your domain with the Web 2.0 applications in place. They have gathered leads for the type of products and services you deal in. You can simply purchase leads from such companies and follow up on them yourself.

Continuity Programs:

With the purchase of a continuity program, you have an Internet marketing strategist on retainer. These individuals offer programs whereby they implement new marketing strategies monthly over a fixed period of time, or they do all the implementation of the strategies at the beginning and simply maintain them over a given period of time.

Some Final Thoughts

Your online marketing strategy is based on getting more potential customers, client and patients to your site and converting them into paid business. It really is that simple. Through using a wide variety of techniques, you can pinpoint those customers and make sure they find your business when they search online for products or services that you provide. When they find your website or other online assets, a variety of other online marketing tools will be waiting to convert them into buying customers.

In order to do this effectively, most of your focus will be on four major aspects of your marketing plan: using keywords in all online content, having a mobile marketing system, creating a 5-star reputation for reviews and having as many quality links and citations as possible to your website. The more 4-star and 5-star reviews, citations and quality backlinks you have, the better your site and other online assets will place in search engine results, and the more people will find your website and trust your business. The more effectively you use keywords, especially on your dedicated mobile website, images and videos, the more search engine-friendly your content is and, therefore, more likely to be ranked.

The more visitors you get to your website, the better your chances will be to get more new customers. New customers mean an increase in sales and profit as previously mentioned when reviewing the potential for exponential growth in online marketing for your business. And more sales and profit means a hight ROI.

Techniques to Increase Your Business's Profits

Whether you have suffered a downturn in your business, have never built it to the level you are aiming for or if you are just starting out, your goal needs to be using online marketing strategies to increase your profits. There are four basic ways to improve profits:

1. Increase customers

    a. Increase traffic to increase customers.

    b. Add to product offerings to make them more compelling.

    c. Use PPC, SEO, local business results, article marketing, etc.

2. Increase number of transactions per customer

    a. Build a mailing list.

    b. Increase customer communications through autoresponders, newsletters and broadcast messages.

    c. Offer them upsell opportunities—pitch something seasonal.

    d. Send out reminders for services and specials.

3. Increase the average dollar amount per transaction

    a. Offer bundle packages and upgrades and stronger reasons to purchase.

4. Decrease costs, finding free traffic, lowering cost per click

    a. Increasing conversions thereby decreasing costs.

    b. Offer a bonus, change a headline or offer a free consultation.

    c. Even improving conversions from 1% to 2% is a 100% improvement and cuts costs for buying traffic in half—pure profit!

By putting an online business plan in place and following through with it, you can achieve all of these goals. You can easily improve your profits through the strategic use of online marketing techniques that will increase customers, increase the number of transactions per customer, increase the average dollar amount per transaction and decrease costs while finding free traffic which leads to a lower cost per click.

Take the time today to investigate if your website is doing all it can to attract new customers for you. If not, get started putting the simple online business plan into place on your own or with the help of a professional.

Get started now on your online business plan to rescue your business with effective marketing. Good Luck! I look forward to being a part of your success story!

All the Very Best-

Your Free Bonus Gift

As a thank-you for purchasing Demystified – The Business Owner's Roadmap to More Customers, Clients and Patients Online, Markus K. Loving is offering a scholarship for you to join his DemystifiedBookOnline.com Online Training Site. That is a total value of $597 – for free!

These guest memberships are available to purchasers of Markus K. Loving's Demystified – The Business Owner's Roadmap to More Customers, Clients and Patients Online. The membership registration must be completed by December 31, 2016 and this offer is made on space available basis. All guest Memberships are first come first serve. To assure your spot, please register immediately at www.DemystifiedBookOnline.com

At Markus' DemystifiedBookOnline.com Training Site, you will build on what you learned in this book by discovering:

- *Facebook Demystified*
- *LinkedIn Demystified*
- *YouTube Demystified*
- *Google My Business Demystified*
- *Press Releases Demystified*
- *Email Marketing Demystified*
- *Text Message Marketing Demystified*
- *Foursquare Demystified*
- *PPC Demystified*
- *Social Media Demystified*
- *Reputation Marketing Demystified*
- *Local SEO Demystified*
- *And So Much More...*

By the end of the course, you will release your inner Online Marketing Guru to achieve true Online Market Domination. Best of all, the strategies you'll have learned will serve your business for years to come.

No matter your current level of online marketing prowess, if you're not totally satisfied with your online success to attract more leads and customers, and you want to feel finally what it's like to go down the Internet road to success, then register for Markus' DemystifiedBookOnline.com Membership Training Site today because...

Isn't it time you received your share of customer from the Internet?

Register now at

www.DemystifiedBookOnline.com

ONLINE MARKETING
DEMYSTIFIED
MEMBERSHIP COURSE
CERTIFICATE

Markus Loving and OMD Training
invite you to join our online training
course, as a complimentary guest. To
Register and for more information,
go to
www.DemystifiedBookOnline.com

Use registration code:

1207180169

* The offer is open to all purchasers of Demystified – The Business Owner's Roadmap to More Customer, Clients and Patients Online by Markus K. Loving. Original proof of purchase is required. The offer is limited to DemystifiedBookOnline.com membership training site only, and your registration for the membership training site is subject to availability of space and /or changes to the program. Corporate or organizational purchaser may not use one book to invite more than two people. While participants will be responsible for registering with accurate information and any other costs, initial 3 months of membership is complimentary. Participants in the membership site are under no additional financial obligation whatsoever to DymystifiedBookOnline.com or Markus K Loving for the first 3 months of membership. Registration on the membership site must be completed by December 31, 2016.

What Business Owners Are Saying...

George Schwabe

Your Insurance Advocate / Industry Public Speaker

Markus has assisted me with various projects. His website and search engine marketing skills are exceptional. He does what he advertises. Google knows who I am, and so does anyone who's looking. I highly recommend him.

Dr. Norman Roth

CEO at Sales Enhancers

Markus is brilliant, he really understands Social Media and how to get the most ROI from it, he is creative, a relationship builder and provides superior value I highly recommend him.

Bruce Himmelblau

Producer & YouTube Content Marketing Strategist at Blue Sky Video Productions

I've gotten to know Markus over the past year and have had the privilege to serve with him on local committees as well as do presentations with him. He is an authority in online marketing and SEO. He helps businesses break through all the noise on the Internet and reach their target audience. From search engines to social media, Markus manages to stay informed and ahead of the curve.

He also takes time to give back to the community where he works, both through seminars on Online Market Domination for businesses and service to non-profit charities.

He is a great strategic partner, and I look forward to working with him more in the future as the Internet and all its components continually changes.

Phil Nocerino

PC Tech at Windys Computer Repairs & Tuning Element Products Dealer

I have known Markus for several years through networking, and he does a great job of taking your business presence on the internet to the next level. I highly recommend him for promoting your business online.

April Toney

Executive Director at Illinois Arborist Association

I have worked with Markus over the past few years. Markus has exceptional website development, social media and marketing skills. Markus also has the utmost integrity and he is always happy to help whenever I call. His customer service skills are top notch! I highly recommend him!

Keith Collins

Attorney At Law

Markus is bright, energetic, and talented. What sets him apart from the crowd is his extraordinary SEO and online marketing experience and expertise

About the Author

Markus K. Loving is the founder & CEO of
OnlineMarketDomination.com.

Since 2007, Markus has empowered companies to become an Authority in their respective fields and Dominate Their Markets Online. He has spoken to thousands of business owners across America and has influenced countless business owners to put their Online Business Plan into action in his workshops and seminars.

Fact: Markus can show your Organization how to get better results with less time, money and effort. He's available for:

- Keynotes & Workshops
- Strategic Marketing Seminars
- Specific Online Marketing Strategy Seminars
- One on One Online Marketing Coaching

A Little Bit About Markus and OnlineMarketDomination.com

In the late 70's Star Wars entered on the big screen, and some of us scratched our heads and asked "What is this all about?", in the 80's there were the big bag phones, Cellular car phones, and PCs, then in the 90's it was the onset of the Internet and the World Wide Web so again people were asking, "What is this all about?" Needless to say the rest is history and as every new Star Wars movie has entered on the scene over the years with great anticipation on the part of its fans, like Markus, so has the world eagerly anticipated what will be the next new thing on the Internet, on our Android/iPhones, on our tablets, that will continue to revolutionize the world of computers and technology, and the little microchips that do so much.

Markus has kept up with the evolution of the computer and Internet acquiring programming skills at the age 10. By college, he had already become proficient in four (4) computer languages and earned college credit before graduating from Glenbrook South High School. Just as with his passion for Star Wars, his passion for computer science and Internet marketing continues to grow. For those of us who think of computers and the Internet as a foreign language, they truly can be, and because of this they need an

expert interpreter to understand them and get the most out of them for those of us who know a fraction of what the expert knows about laptops, PC's, search engines, social media and many of the dynamic uses that can be optimized through someone who understands its expansive capabilities.

One of his other passions, in health and nutrition, lead him to develop a sales and distribution company for over 15 years which at the height was doing $15M a month in sales. It was in these "trenches" that he developed his keen sense of marketing, sales, public speaking, recruiting, training and general business acumen to understand what's needed to increase the bottom line.

With his most recent #1 Best Selling Book, "Demystified – The Business Owner's Roadmap to Getting More Customers, Clients and Patients Online." he has given us a tool we can take and maximize our online authority and presence, which translates into more business for all of us.

Markus has the right formula for small businesses like yours to give you the competitive edge to go up against the bigger companies. He has taken many businesses to greater heights with strategic marketing campaigns, 5-star reputation marketing and mobile marketing systems. A leader throughout the business community, he brings to bear his expertise to give you the strategies and implementations of what your business needs. "The first page is where business happens" & "Why compete when you can dominate?" is Online Market Domination's core philosophy. The World Wide Web is here to stay and to take over the world, make sure you're getting your share of it.

Call Online Market Domination Today (847) 238-2768!

Happily married, Markus resides in the Chicago Area with his wife and his daughter who is his shining star, pride and joy, and excels in Dancing, Acting and All Star Cheerleading. So when he's not helping companies dominate their markets online, he's enjoying taking lots of pictures and videos of his family.

Notes:

Notes:

Notes:

Notes:

23027650R00065

Made in the USA
Columbia, SC
07 August 2018